Diary of a Twin Flame

The True Story of a Spiritual Transformation

By Alex A Adams

Introduction

Have you ever encountered someone with whom you immediately connected? You could see who they were at their core, share a quirky sense of humour, and exchange knowing glances that conveyed thoughts only the two of you understood?

As you got to know each other better, you discovered even more similarities. Maybe you both secretly adored 1950s rock and roll or had a hidden fondness for anchovies. Congratulations, you've encountered a soul mate, and I wish you all the happiness and success in the world.

However, this story isn't about soul mates; it's about meeting your twin flame. When I shared my plan to write this with someone close to me, their response was, "You're a better artist than a writer." That comment pretty much sums up what it means to be a twin: persisting despite life's challenges. What happens to us is beyond belief, and while I'll use pseudonyms to protect identities, everything I'm about to share is absolutely true. No embellishments, just raw reality, if you are a twin, many things here will resonate. But remember we are all different and have different experiences, the outcome however, tends to be the same.

All too often the media glorifies twin flames, mistaking it for a romantic relationship on steroids. We see quirky celebrities claiming to be twin flames, even Taylor swift mentions the twin flame bruise, bruise ? More like the twin flame wood chipper !

Whilst deciding how to write this, part of me wanted to spare you the trauma of what i went through, part of my ego feels a little embarrassed, my actions as a grown man with worldly wisdom, baffled and embarrassed me, even at the time.

I've left out details of what the company does, whilst it is a pivotal aspect of the story, what I did isn't important in the scheme of things.

Some things will become clearer later on as I backjump times and marry them up with experiences. But with advice, I thought it better to take you along the journey as I experienced it.

I will embellish on much of it later, and as to what twins are for and so on. Let's just say, things escalate.

When I refer to god, it's for want of a better word, but you could say the creator, allah, source, the universe, the force, spirit. It is not the Christian god so many have been indoctrinated with. I remember only too well my own reaction when looking at the word god. It was a precursor to be preached to, scolded for all my wrongs, and something about being smited.

Life Was Good

I'd heard girlfriends talk about soulmates, and I'd nod politely, but I didn't give it much thought. While I knew there was more to life than meets the eye, I also understood that we had to navigate this existence as best we could and savor every moment. Did God exist? Was there an afterlife? Well, it didn't seem to matter much. After all, we weren't handed a rulebook when we arrived here, and the Bible seemed riddled with contradictions. Who could say what was right? Perhaps this whole experience is a cosmic game played by two alien teenagers lounging on their alien couch, eating alien crisps.

I occasionally pondered the meaning of life, but for the most part, I simply dove into life headfirst and got on with it. I would have described myself as spiritual, but it was mostly to appear cool and open-minded, especially while indulging in less-than-virtuous activities. I had had what could be called unexplained encounters before all of this, but what it meant? I didn't know.

I was a well-known figure in my local community, having built a successful business with a turnover in the millions. I owned a comfortable home in town and a brand new BMW 4x4. As a man, I measured my worth by my achievements. I didn't shy away from mentioning my successes, but I tried to do so without sounding boastful. I genuinely appreciated where hard work, and admittedly a bit of luck, had brought me. I took pride in offering advice and assistance to those who were also building their own dreams. I held deep admiration for fellow entrepreneurs who put in the effort and weathered the storms that often came their way. In short, I was proud of what I had achieved, not arrogant, but not falsely humble either. Though admittedly I sometimes strayed across the line of humility.

I lived with my girlfriend Karen, who was 13 years my junior, which was not unusual for me. Karen also worked for me. I had always been drawn to younger women, even before I had money. I considered myself young at heart, and I believed I looked younger than my age. Our relationship was strong, and it showed. We discussed our future, children and shared goals. We seemed to be in perfect sync, understanding each other's quirks and tolerating our darker sides. We genuinely enjoyed each other's company and had a lot of fun together. I felt like I had found my future wife, and life was exceptionally good. I wouldn't have changed a thing about it. Karen often spoke of us being soulmates, of our past lives together, and how she saw me (as in saw my soul). Honestly, I didn't feel the same way, but I found it endearing that she believed in such things. After all, who was I to definitively say if they were true or not? For me though, it sounded like nonsense. I did, however, love her, or certainly I believed so.

Sarah

That's where I was in life when Sarah joined the company. I was content and genuinely happy with everything in my life. I felt at peace, like a fully integrated member of society, and I had found the woman I wanted to spend the rest of my life with. There were no doubts in my mind.

I didn't personally interview Sarah; the company had grown to a size where I often didn't know the names of my employees, and I rarely interacted with those below middle management. Sarah was one such case. We didn't talk, but I certainly noticed her presence. It wasn't an immediate attraction, though she was attractive, no love-at-first-sight scenario. Our eyes never met, and as a mature and happily committed man, I had enough self-control not to pay much attention to the odd passing fancy anyway. It was just that there was something intriguing about her. It felt like I could see a glimpse of her soul, yet neither of us acknowledged each other's existence.

It was even before we spoke that I was absolutely certain Sarah had been a part of a previous life, this was the first time I had ever felt anything like this. Even though I wasn't sure of such things, I just knew this down to my core. This was the first time I'd ever experienced anything like this, it was very strange. I instinctively knew that her and I would share something together again in this life. Though what? I had no idea.

It's only in hindsight that I realised my relationship began to deteriorate around the time Sarah joined the company. There was nothing from my part that was less committed, there was nothing I could definitively say was the cause of the decline. Karen started to be unfaithful, and my old ways began to creep back into my mind. My old ways were nights of drinking, scoring coke and maybe shacking up with the nearest willing woman. Still, apart from the odd moment, I felt this relationship could be salvaged, and we were due to go on the holiday of a lifetime before we both agreed to start a family. As a wise soul I figured we were both having our last little blasts. I wasn't so twistedly jealous of what she was getting up to, basically because I was getting up to pretty much the same thing. Still it hurt at times, and I certainly wish it hadn't gone that way.

The Company Gets Sold

About the same time, a competitor approached me with an offer to buy a portion of my company (My company had two distinct areas of operation). This was his second attempt, and while I had easily rebuffed him before, this time it became evident that I needed to take some action. My business had grown to a turnover of 7 million, but as the saying goes, "Turnover is vanity." The stark reality was that my business was at risk of decline if I didn't sell or secure funds from another source.

And so we agreed on a price, it was higher than I thought it was worth, and only sentiment pulled a few heart strings of doubt. Otherwise it was a good deal. One of the caveats of this deal however, none of the employees working on that part of the business could work for me for three years. I had already made a list of employees and their salaries before the deal was struck.

Well this caveat included Sarah, and when the deal was done and became public knowledge (it was in the local paper, since both our companies were known locally) her name was on the list. However there was no way on God's green Earth I was going to let Sarah go for three years. It was being faced with this reality I was suddenly aware of just how drawn I was to her.

Now to be clear, my business employed many very good looking young women, that was just the type of business it was. I was used to being surrounded by attractive women, so it was far more than being attracted to someone's looks. I'm not perfect but nor am I a rat ready to run up every drainpipe in town.

This was when we first spoke, she was bashful in front of me, and instantly I could sense there was something between us. Though being as professional as I possibly could be, I explained that she needed to hand in her notice that day, I needed her resignation in writing and that when the company was sold she could come back and join the other portion of the company that remained with me.

This she did without hesitation, and it appeared with complete trust.

I handed my counterpart the list of names that would be coming over and explained that unfortunately Sarah had got another job. I brushed it off as if she wasn't really that important anyway. But the simple fact is, she was starting to be the only thing on my mind. And I didn't know why.

The First Kiss

It was the very day after the company sold, I remember the date well of course. It had been a stressful process, and I saw it as a turning point in being able to resurrect the relationship between Karen and I. No more messing about. I was willing to forgive her trespasses, and I was willing to stop mine. I texted her that it had all gone through, money was in the bank. She was at home, I was expecting her to say *let's celebrate", "let's go out", "let's do something". Instead all I got was one word. "Awesome"

A word she used all the time for everything, "put sugar in my tea? "Awesome". It meant nothing. And it felt like it meant nothing. I knew our relationship was over. I was netting nearly half a million, Karen worked for me and lived with me, yet she seemed as indifferent as if I'd have said I was getting mushrooms for dinner.

But what I've come to learn about this whole thing, is nothing is by chance, literally nothing. No matter how random things are there always seems to be a reason. And I wouldn't find out this reason until 10 years later.

Well, with that one word text I decided to take the remainder of staff out for drinks, a common occurrence. Sarah was messing about with one of the other guys who worked for me, who was I to get jealous? Karen worked with me after all and I certainly couldn't show any outward sentiment of attraction. I was able to be very level headed most of the time despite my own emotions. I don't like to think my emotions rule my thoughts. I assumed they had gone off in another group of workers.

Sarah joined us at the pub, having left the group she was with along with the fellow she was involved with. It's important to mention that Sarah was also in a relationship and was openly displaying her involvement with her co-worker, which was not something I would typically admire. She seemed to be leading this guy along, and it was evident that he was infatuated with her, while for her, it appeared to be more of a game than anything else.

As the evening went on we decided to go back to the office. Karens text still stung, she didnt care if I was out all night. We made the phone calls and went back to the office with carry outs and other substances.

Sarah was intoxicated, and this was the first time she had actually made an effort to chat with me, her bare feet curling up on the desk I was sitting on, her big eyes flickering up at me, yeah I can see through that shite, but inside I just couldn't help but be so drawn to her. She complained about her ex, about how she worked three jobs to support her ex. Normally this would have looked like a May Day parade to me. There were that many red flags. But again, all I cared about was that she was flirting with me.

As the night wore on, I couldn't ignore the strong attraction I felt towards Sarah. Outwardly, I tried to flirt with another girl, but it was strange how little control I seemed to have over my emotions. Even amidst the haze of substances, this feeling was so overpowering that it almost sobered me up. I can remember most of that evening quite vividly, even to this day.

It reached 2 am, I can't quite recall the exact sequence of events that led to Sarah and me briefly being alone outside the office, where others were still present, but there we were. I couldn't resist the impulse. I leaned in and kissed her.

I was hooked, I didn't care about her fling with her co-worker, I just wanted her. And though the night was messy, in the end Sarah left, that was after we went elsewhere to someone's flat, my aims less than carnal. Later on she said she hated me that evening. She had a funny way of showing it.

Relationship Ends

And that was that, Sarah left the company. I again tried to resurrect the relationship with Karen, but I may as well have tried holding a tea party for the dead. Although we did go on our amazing holiday, it was hollow. I had nothing left in me, the last time we slept together was on that holiday.

I was gutted to be honest, I had truly thought we were meant to be, I doubted my own instincts as well. I had always wanted kids, a family of my own. My own family, having been a mitigating disaster zone, spread all over the place. Dad was dead anyway, the closest person to me was my Grandmother. My Brother didn't speak to me, I just wanted a haven where I could find people I loved and that loved me back. That dream seemed to disappear with the relationship that was lost.

Still, I was well rid of Karen, she was two faced, and had become a rather unpleasant person to be around, according to others she was strutting her stuff around other girls in the company. And whilst Sarah wasn't out of my mind she was no more than a passing fancy, one that I knew to stay away from, romantically speaking. She was trouble. Not only that, but at almost 15 years my junior? Yeah, I wanted someone a bit older now.

Second Contact

S arah was no slouch in her job, and I did genuinely believe she would be good for the company, so the next move wouldn't have happened had she been no good. I wasn't that shallow. As promised I contacted her again, four months after she had officially resigned. We met and she agreed to join up again as we had discussed. She had some trepidation as in this section of the company she had no experience with, however I knew her skills were transferable so I had no such doubts. Karen still worked with me as well, and whilst I was ok with our seperation she still seemed to have issues, even though it was her idea.

Working with Karen wasn't always smooth sailing, but she was good at her job, and we managed to maintain a professional relationship. Despite the occasional argument, I made an effort to remain as professional as possible, and we got along fine. Credit to Karen, we did openly communicate with each other. For the most part, we handled our separation like adults.

To provide context for what transpired next, it's important to know that I was still owed £100,000 from the sale of my previous company. I was determined to collect this money without any hindrances, including potential contract violations.

Consequently, I wanted to keep it a secret that Sarah was rejoining my company, as I had removed her name from the list of employees who were not allowed to work with me again. And I knew very well that any excuse not to hand over that money would have been taken.

I had received information from another employee, one who was usually level-headed, that they had seen Sarah at a party. Apparently, she had been quite intoxicated and had openly told everyone that she was coming back to work with me. Her announcement wasn't discreet at all. In the town we lived in, word had a way of spreading, despite it not being a particularly small town. Over 250k. People simply loved to gossip, and I was a known figure in the community. I reacted swiftly by sending her an angry text message, as I had explicitly instructed her not to broadcast her return. I essentially warned her that if she continued to spread this information, I wouldn't be rehiring her. I felt hurt as well, as my trust had been breached. In hindsight, it may seem like an overreaction over a seemingly small matter, but at the time, that £100,000 was crucial to me.

She apologised. I said we had better meet up, as on text I was less than subtle. Though I was cross I didn't want it to appear that I was absolutely livid, after all, there wasn't any way I'd actually carry out any threat of not hiring her. We agreed to meet up in a local pub. I won't go into details, but within 5 hours we were in bed. There was just nothing that could stop us. The next morning she ran, literally out of the blue she just ran out the house. I was dazed, but thought it for the best as she was trouble and I knew it.

Sarah joined the company, and as expected she did well. I tried to keep   everything as professional as possible, there wasn't any strangeness, though every now and then Sarah and I would end up sleeping together. A situation that was fine by me, I had no intention of having another relationship with a coworker and someone much younger than me.

Sarah had joined in March, she was now single, as the year went on we ended up together more and more. We usually went to the pub, had a few drinks, called one in and ended up back at my place. It almost seemed as if we did this whilst under the influence we could pretend that it was just a bit of fun. In reality I was falling more and more. I could have married her and had babies on the spot. Even though logically that would have been a bad idea.

The Light Within

One night as we were chatting, she was sitting on the kitchen counter. I put my hand on her chest, it was something I've just been able to do for some reason, I can kind of sense people. (Girls anyway not guys, never tried it with guys) I rested my hand on her chest, and it simply felt like the most beautiful thing I've ever felt, it was like a light within her, a glow, a serenity, it felt like love. One thing is certain. I immediately fell in love with her then and there, and nothing could have stopped that. This wasn't something that could be faked, not something that could be mustered within, it wasn't a trick of my senses, this was pure connection. Even to this day I can still recall the beauty of what I felt. It was just so pure, like a glowing star in pure water. Whether she felt it as well I don't know. We just smiled at each other. Something I'll never forget. It truly felt amazing. For a moment I had a glimpse of true love, just a moment. But it was enough.

Still, I tried my level best not to let myself get carried away. Sarah was still not great relationship material, I'd already seen how readily she would flaunt other relationships behind her boyfriends back. Not a pleasant thing to do. Regardless, I had enough self confidence. I felt I could manage things, but I also felt kind of intimidated, not by her, but by my own feelings.

As I look back on those days, I recall nearly nothing of the business, something I had been building for years, something I was proud of, something that defined me. I was still turning over £3m or so, we were still a force within our industry, but I started to stop caring.

As Christmas approached Sarah and I had to go away on business, this was with a few others so not just us. We had booked separate rooms, but of course we ended up in the same room. I'll never forget waking up with her arms holding onto me tight, it felt like the most wonderful place in the world. I just kept falling more and more.

However, us being together on this trip had ended up getting back to Karen. I no longer really cared what she thought, but part of me almost wanted to get back with her, it was safe, my feelings for her were normal, not off the damn charts like they were with Sarah. I told Sarah Karen knew, her sharp response was simply "I don't care" wow, I thought, this was a really sharp response from someone who had so often seemed so feminine and pretended to be scared of life. I was looking out for her, yet she didn't seem to give a shit, and even shunned me for mentioning it.

No matter what I did though, I couldn't get away from this magnetic pull towards Sarah, it was wearing me down, trying to fight it was hard and going with it was scary, I felt vulnerable, I didn't want her to ever see just how much of a hold she had on me, quite frankly I didn't trust her, and with good reason.

But damn the consequences, what I felt for her was too strong to ignore. And not one to do nothing, well I decided to take things forward and see what happened.

Nervously, I asked if she'd like to go on holiday with me, to my surprise she agreed, I had felt like a teenager asking a girl to dance for the first time. It was nerve wracking, and that surprise "You would??" Feeling took me back to when I was younger. I felt kind of stupid. Here I was this supposedly confident business owner asking an employee to go on holiday.

This kind of opened things up for us and we started seeing more of each other, even sleeping together sober, she had even said she would have a baby with me. Strangely it was the exact same time as I was thinking the exact same thing in my head, I dare not to imagine this again after the last let down. But honestly, I could have got her pregnant there and then and been fine with it. Even looking back now, I don't think it would have been a silly idea, even though it probably would have been.

It was then her ex had had a house fire and asked to stay at her place. We weren't "official" so there wasn't much I could say, but you can guess I was less than pleased. It was under these circumstances that I picked her up from her place, knowing her ex was there to go on holiday together. It felt shit.

Sweden

We embarked on a trip to Sweden and Finland, and the landscapes were absolutely breathtaking. However, during the journey, I noticed that Sarah started to withdraw. It seemed like the weight of expectations had taken a toll on her. She contributed very little, and I won't deny that it hurt. The atmosphere became tense and far from enjoyable. The more I tried to connect, the more I felt pushed away. It became increasingly clear to me that this was not going to work.

When we returned home, I made the decision that this relationship wasn't going anywhere. I questioned whether what I felt for her was genuine or just lust. After all, I was 40 years old, and whilst I was a red-blooded male, I wasn't a teenager with an infatuation. We didn't have a sit-down conversation about it; I simply tried to distance myself. But inevitably, we ended up at the pub, calling one in, and ended up back in bed.

We talked about the holiday, and it was then Sarah opened up about feelings of inadequacy, not being good enough and so on. Well as far as I'm concerned we all battle with those feelings from time to time, but just get on with it. And certainly my own trepidation when it came to us wasn't far off what she was talking about. As usual we seemed to feel the same thing at the same time. Only we handled it differently.

Gradually, we began to open up more, even though a year had passed since we started this confusing push-and-pull dynamic. We still didn't fully open up to each other, and Sarah had an oddly disconcerting effect on me. She made me nervous, but in an intriguing way. Strangely enough, she felt the same about me. It was as if we were both holding something back, and in truth I absolutely was holding a lot back. My immense feelings and love. It would spill out into manipulative behavior at times. Something I wasn't proud of.

We still tried to have some sort of relationship, and embarked on another trip, this time it was just too intense and Sarah eventually said things were not going to work out. I was broken hearted to hear her say that, but agreed, and it was true. And with that, we had sex.

As different as we were to each other there was just something exactly the same, during the push pull dynamic we both even agreed that inside we are the same, I had no idea what it actually meant though. Sarah had broken things off, but in honesty I'm not sure what changed, even looking back there's no line between when we sort of dated, and when we didn't. I couldn't even call her an ex.

It was 2013, and my mind was on Sarah, far more than it was the business, it was then things started to slip with the business. Because my attention had been elsewhere we had got ourselves into a pickle, and yes directly because I wasn't paying attention.

There was a choice, sell my house to get us out of the mess or accept the business failure and walk away with my house? Well if the business went that meant Sarah would as well, and here I was faced with the fact that I knew if Sarah didn't have a reason to see me, she wouldn't. And yes I sold my house, not to save the business. But because nothing mattered more than being with Sarah. And I tried not admitting that to myself at the time, I pretended it was to save other jobs, the business would recover, I could buy another house anyway. All of which was a lie. I worked hard for that house, I loved it, in all my years I never had anywhere I could call home, just that one place. Even today I think of that house I owned for five years as my only home I ever had.

Two years passed, we still spent lots of time together, we still slept together, I was with her on all her jobs, all the time. She wouldn't do them without me. I started to resent being there for her all the time yet receiving pretty much no gratitude for it. She in turn resented the fact that I was still close to her in the workplace and she didn't want anything to do with that. Our cocaine use gradually got out of hand.

It was a push pull dynamic we couldn't break, well certainly I couldn't, I tried to think about dating another girl that I knew from the past, she liked me as well. But this didn't even last the night, I just wanted her gone. I missed Sarah all the time I was with this other girl. I couldn't even be bothered sleeping with her.

I knew this was unhealthy. We talked about going to Vegas and just getting married, part of me was actually serious. I felt stuck. I was hopelessly in love, like so much in love I wanted nothing else other than to be with her. To call ourselves Girlfriend and Boyfriend just seemed twee and silly. In fact, to call it anything is impossible. It just was.

One time I recall just after we had been together, lying on the floor Sarah said she loved me, but those feelings of love were just chemicals in her brains, it wasn't real, that stung, though was she in the same place I was? In love but in self denial as well. For my part I had no such doubts, I was in deep, I'm not even sure there's a word for the feelings I felt. Love coupled with rage and self hatred.

But at the same time, being with Sarah was like home, I never wanted to be anywhere else, I was just happy being near her, not like a puppy, not like some lost soul. But in a way I felt whole when around her, I felt like more. It just felt right. Something I've never felt before. I always felt I had to prove myself, be this or that, and whilst the dynamic was tense, it was also familiar. It's really hard to explain.

Karen got married during this time, she had been seeing a drummer of a band my company had hired. I had no doubt she was seeing him whilst we were together, I didn't care in the slightest. I still recall Sarah asking me on the day of her wedding. How do you feel? I said "nothing" and that was the truth. The woman I was planning to spend my life with was getting married, and it may as well have been the next door neighbour. I literally didn't give two shits whatsoever. How could I ? When I was with the person that meant more than the twee institution of marriage. This felt bigger, so much bigger.

We went on another holiday, this one as disastrous as the last, we'd been around each other almost three years, yet the tension again was palpable. I was exhausted, hurt, almost broken. I hated how much I loved her, resented the fact that she must have known and I felt used. Hated the fact I felt too weak and powerless to do anything about it. It was a horrible situation. Probably for both of us as well. But then she was not past walking away if she wanted to.

First Ending

We walked into my place, our usual cocaine in hand, after the pub, I was on the phone. Sarah just got up and walked out, not a word, she just walked. I knew that was that, not a word was spoken between us the next day either. We didn't need to. And to be honest one of us needed to walk, this was an insane dynamic. There was no way I could have. It just had such a hold on me. We still however spent time together, mainly for work purposes. But I felt that for both of us that was just an excuse to be around each other.

It had been four years we had been around each other, push pull, neither of us being faithful in particular, but for me I had absolutely no way of ever wanting another woman, so I ended up going with ladies if ill repute, it suited my cocaine habit, dark and comforting. Sarah went on tinder. I was in such a mess anyway, I'm not sure what I felt anymore.

I needed to sort out my cocaine habit, it had gotten out of hand, not a few days would go by without me getting some in. I was an addict, and I knew it. After one too many disgraceful nights I dragged myself along to an anonymous meeting. No longer could I pretend I was better than anyone else, I was a mess, hiding it as best as possible from the world, but honestly, the world didn't care either way.

At cocaine anonymous I found redemption, I had been using cocaine on and off for years, heavily since I started being around Sarah, unable to face my own feelings sober. It was here I finally got clean, and for the first time I was faced with God. I was less interested in the God thing than I was in making new friends, I genuinely had fun with my new sober pals. The obsession with Sarah didn't leave me, but it became manageable. She would still do things to hurt me, or should i say I got hurt when I felt spurned, no doubt I hurt her back.

But the fact is, for the first time in years It felt like life was turning around, I felt great, I prayed just as I was told, and it seemed to work. I had no idea how, but it did. Yes, this was definitely down to being sober but as I prayed everything began to feel lighter. A darkness lifted from me.

The Big Push

It was Sarah's idea for our new big push for the company. Others were on board, including Karen. In honesty I had thought about a similar idea, the company hadn't properly recovered from almost going bust in 2013 the industry kept on changing, as many do in this ever increasing digital age, barely five years go by without some new technological advance putting rest to more sectors of a once thriving industrial area.

It was the new big push for this new idea, everyone was on board with the idea. We gave it our all, as we entered 2016 with a new vigour everything seemed to start going our way again. I had renewed focus on the business, a sober and clear vision of the future. And initially things started to go well, Sarah and I spent a bit more time together, and it was again pleasant to be around her. But then things started falling apart, we got into the local papers, bad news on the front page, false news as well, but it scuppered our plans, we were also too far down the line to stop, or it was certainly curtains.

The more sober I got the more I healed. Sarah seemed to start losing her mind, and I knew the two were connected but I had no idea how. Then her mum emigrated, and things just got worse. But yet we continued with the push ahead with the big plan. I was still always there for Sarah, when she started losing it at the pub I went home with her, stayed the night to comfort her. I loved her dearly, but the fact is what could I do? I couldn't spend the rest of my life at the beck and call someone who didn't reciprocate. I wasn't a teenager anymore, I had told her this, but to no avail, she still wanted me around. And I wanted to be around her as well. My feelings for her just kept bursting at the seams inside me, it was almost impossible to contain, and I started resenting the fact I felt she was taking advantage of that fact.

And Then She's Gone

On the day of a major marketing push, news of the passing of one of Sarah's old friends added another layer of emotional turmoil. The weight of this loss, combined with the challenges we were already facing, sent Sarah into a deep emotional struggle, and I too felt the impact. While I harboured a secret realisation that the business was on the brink of collapse, I continued with the marketing push, uncertain of what else to do.

Sarah attended her friend's funeral, and in the midst of everything, I began to lose my own sense of stability. My emotions for her surged uncontrollably, pouring out in a chaotic mix of anger, resentment, hate, love, and compassion. Love, in its true form, isn't just a pleasant, soft feeling; it has the power to unearth and expose all the complex emotions within you. It starts by pushing out the negative feelings, and I was grappling with a mix of fear and love that seemed incompatible at the time.

Sarah had promised to be at the marketing push the next day, and even though I didn't expect her, when she asked not to go that morning, something in me acted involuntarily. I can't explain it, but I started texting her angry texts. This wasn't the first time of course, having done this plenty of times before to my shame. But this was out of my control, I was texting with tears down my face, barely holding onto sanity, like a force taking me over. I could feel her pain as well and the more I felt it, the more I tried to stop, but I just couldn't.

This had to stop, I was worried Sarah was going to literally kill herself, the energies between us were horrendous, that day with the team I could think of nothing else but her, and us, and our sanity. I was out of answers. We were both broken. Utterly broken, I was shaking, on my knees with no answers.

Then on Monday I did the only thing left to me. I prayed, on my cycle ride that morning I prayed and prayed, I kept praying, I couldn't hide it from myself. I loved her so much I didn't care anymore what happened to me, I just wanted her to be ok, the energies between us were unmanageable. We couldn't go on like this, I couldn't bear losing her, but at least please god help me not make things worse for her, give me the strength to accept anything that needs to happen for her to be ok.

Then I heard a voice.

The voice said "if you believe what you are saying ride down this alleyway"

OK that was strange, did I just hear that? Was it in my head? Am I imagining this ?

But I did as was asked of me, it felt rather strange to be honest, slightly embarrassing, but still, she was more important than my feelings.

At the end of the alleyway I looked to the sun, and said again, help her, no matter what the outcome, help her.

Then the voice asked "are you sure?'

With the "are you sure" I knew two things, one my life was about to take a massive hit, and two, Sarah would be ok. It meant losing her. I knew that, as much as I almost couldn't face it, I knew it was for the best.

It's hard to describe how I knew these things, it was like, in an instant I had some sort of knowing. That's the best way I can describe it.

I replied.

"Yes"

Then the simple reply of.

"Ok"

And with that I felt the world come back to normal, sounds were crisper, colours brighter, and more importantly I felt so so much better. I felt able to be better for her, able to take some control of my energy which seemed to be spilling out all over the place.

I wasn't sure what had happened, were those voices in my head? it certainly didn't sound like my voice, but regardless it seemed to have worked. Well something had happened anyway.

To try and explain the voice I always use the idea of a very good waiter at a restaurant where you are in well over your head, and you can't understand the menu. Your waiter is acting as your servant. But he's also your guide and indeed your master. It's his realm but you are welcomed. It's a soft and comforting voice. But also powerful and certain.

I went to work, it was ten past nine. Andy, an employee who'd been with me for years , asked "Where's Sarah ?" And with that I knew I'd never see Sarah again.

"She's gone," I told Andy, my heart sinking.

"Don't be silly, she's probably just running late," he replied.

This was what I had asked for. I also knew she would be okay. Sarah had sent me a cryptic email message. She had completely fallen apart and had to call in sick, while I had managed to pull myself together. It seemed like fate had made her worse. I knew she was gone for good, but I couldn't help but worry about her.

The email didn't seem like her style, and another employee suggested that she might be playing games and using me. That thought did cross my mind, especially since she had posted a coherent message on Facebook assuring her friends that she was okay. I had posted on her Facebook wall, asking where she was and if she was alright. Something I may not have done for anyone else. But I was worried sick.

Sarah was gone, and what ensured was now pure unpleasantness from her to me, the e-mails her mother sent implied everything was my fault. Yet her emigration had been the turning point in Sarah's sanity, I had been the only one to try and be there for her, I was possibly the only one that knew what she was going through. Basically, because I was going through the same myself. And I was in all manner of shit, barely holding on, losing everything I'd worked for all my life. And here I am taking the shit, my e-mails rebuffed and ignored. Oh, the fucking irony!

When Sarah inevitably handed in her notice, another wave of pain hit me, deep and searing. I had seen it coming, but that didn't make it hurt any less.

I was in deep trouble, barely hanging on, and my entire world was collapsing with no one to turn to. Sarah had always been there, her mere presence had been a comfort. Now it felt like my soul was being torn from within me. What was happening? We hadn't been together in a year, yet this final parting tore me apart like nothing I had ever experienced before.

The business started falling apart at the seams, I was falling apart again, this time properly, the brief rest bite I received went, and quickly I started relapsing. The project fell over very publicly. I was in the papers. My face front page, fuck it, I didn't care.

The Fall

My heart and soul had been invested in my business for over 15 years, and it was now teetering on the brink of collapse. This enterprise, for which I had endured times of hunger and financial strain, persisted through the challenges of 9/11, the crash of 2008, and even involved last-minute walks to suppliers to ensure cheques wouldn't bounce whilst I juggled cash. In its construction, I faced adversity, theft, betrayal, gossip, and double-crossing – yet, none of these setbacks deterred me from reaching my destination. On my journey, I extended assistance to countless others, forming both allies and adversaries, and earning both respect and ridicule. Despite the trials, the ultimate objective remained a prize worthy of the toil.

I had always been a shrewd operator, adept at getting out of tight spots, and I did my utmost to salvage what remained of it. For a while it looked as though we may come out of this, battered and bruised, but with a business still intact. It was really the only thing I had left in my life. And what little fight I had left I mustered up to try and save what I could.

The year 2016 was pure hell all the way through. There were hardly three consecutive days where I felt anything close to good. Meanwhile, Sarah's Facebook started to show her enjoying life again. It was nothing short of a miraculous recovery as soon as she quit. I felt played and manipulated, as some other coworkers had warned me that she would do exactly that—take as much as she could from me and then quit. I felt rather foolish, feeling that I had been used all those years. I knew she felt nothing for me at all, and the love I had for her had been in vain. It felt like all my life's effort had been for naught, and I was left with nothing but debt and public humiliation.

My mind drifted back to a comment Sarah once made, about how she enjoyed ruining people's lives. Well, she had certainly succeeded in ruining mine. Yet, despite everything, I still loved her, still cared for her, no matter what. And for that, I couldn't help but hate myself.

The last time I saw Sarah was on a cold December day a few months after she had left. Fate, as it often does with twins, had a hand in the encounter. I usually drove home, but that day, I had to walk because my car was at home. As I walked, my head hung low, trying to hold back tears, it became clear that very day that all my efforts to salvage what remained of my business were in vain. Everything was truly lost, and I wasn't even sure how I was going to pay everyone.

Then we literally almost bumped into each other, Sarah attempted avoiding me by crossing the road. I called out to her, and she turned around with a cross and angry tone, asking, "WHAT?" All I could think of was the last time I had seen her, how much trouble she had been in. I asked if she was okay, and her response was an agitated, "I'M FINE!" I couldn't find the words to speak; if I had, I would have broken down. Instead, I managed a weak smile and a wave, bidding her goodbye. She turned away in anger and continued on her way.

This is something that the older twin will often encounter when we fall. No safety net, no compassion from anyone else. Even from our counterpart. It feels like the universe comes crashing down ruthlessly.

That night broke me, I wanted to just walk away from everything, inside I was done. I lay on the couch shaking, falling apart even more than I ever knew possible. How I managed to go on after that day I still don't know.

Sarah moved away shortly afterwards, back to London, just like I predicted she would eight months beforehand.

But this isn't the end; it's just the beginning. This, my friends, is about to get interesting.

The Dark Night of The Soul

It's only looking back that I knew what was going on, but parts of who I was started falling away, I was lost, confused, and in some ways scared. A far cry from the ever-confident problem solver I prided myself on being. I would spend the evenings just lying on the sofa, stunned, occasionally breaking down. Even alone I was ashamed to shed a tear. I was tougher than this. Having fended for myself since I was 16, this couldn't beat me. But it was.

The dark night of the soul is not something you can easily explain, but it's different from depression, or feeling the blues, your world literally collapses. Like parts of you are falling away, your built persona, everything you once took for granted is questioned.

Friends would start falling away, people take a wide berth as you walk about in a kind of daze, still trying to cling onto the reality of life. You start to see that the person you thought you were was attached to things outside yourself, you are faced with your own frailties and failings as a human.

I would talk to people about the loss of Sarah, for me it was confusing, maybe talking would help? It didn't, "just get over it" people would say. If only it was that simple. Why on Earth was this affecting me so much? It was during this time I had fleeting memories of past lives, one in particular where I was living in the 14th Century Holy Roman Empire in what is now Austria, not too far from Salzburg. I was a village handyman. I recall my wife cooking Stollen bread in big thick iron skillets. In another I recall being a Mesopotamian soldier, this is only a brief vision. And yes it was as strange to me thinking it, or rather envisaging it, as it is for you to read it. Why was I seeing these things ? Was I just going insane ?

This seems common amongst twins, I can't prove beyond a doubt what I was remembering was past lives, but I had the feeling that this life was somehow connected to past lives, maybe I was making up karma?

It was under this backdrop I continued running the business to its inevitable demise in 2016. Those last 6 months of 2016 and first six of 2017 were utter hell. And months I never want to repeat.

Starting Again

After the business failure I managed to salvage some clients and re kindle another business. A few faithful employees stayed with me. Angela in particular, we hadn't been that close, but she was a trusted manager, and as it happened, I actually fired her a few years back for being a little wayward, a mistake on my part, that I thankfully had the chance to rectify.

When the final parts of the business fell I was yet again in the papers, public disgrace complete. It was massive industry news. The front page of big industry papers. But by this time no amount of battering really made that much of a difference.

I had moved accommodation as well, I needed to get every memory of Sarah from my mind and carry on with life. And as it happens life did indeed seem to get better, I stopped feeling the agonising pain of her departure. 2017 looked like it was actually going to be a better year than I thought.

The mess of the old company still lingered and there was that to sort out, but all in all things chugged along as best as could be expected. In fact, by the summer of 2017 things felt good again, after 18 months of hell I wasn't sure that was ever going to happen. This was one tunnel where there seemed to be no light at the end.

The Beast Rears Its Head

My mother had come to visit, and we decided to take a leisurely stroll along one of the quaint lanes near my home. Along one of these charming lanes, we stumbled upon a shop that offered tarot readings. Now, I can read tarot cards myself, as it's been a skill passed down in the family for years. However, it's something I rarely do, and I have no idea how it works. Still, it was my mother's idea to go in and get a reading, so we did.

During the reading, it came up that I would reunite with someone who had moved away, among other things. I couldn't help but think, "Really?" I thought I had been getting over Sarah, yet here I was, faced with a slim chance presented by a shop tarot reader, and I found myself feeling those old emotions of hope and fear all over again. That's how delicate my recovery was.

Just this one thing let a floodgate of emotions come flying back again. Christ almighty was this ever going to leave me? What was going on? This isn't normal to be over something then it just comes flying back again.

I did the one thing I never thought I'd ever do, or in fact. ever need to do. I sought help. I found a counsellor, in fact I found two. One was all but utterly useless, I think he thought I was mad. The other though, had a spiritual edge to her, I liked that, because this wasn't normal.

A few sessions with the counsellor, and she seemed at a loss as well, I wasn't showing signs of abnormal codependency, I was quite lucid and logical about things. I had taken a fall in life, but I was getting back up and dealing with it. Just this thing with Sarah made no sense. It was a year since she had bolted, two years since we even slept together. Yet I was still in all manner of mess over this one thing.

I did research into why I was so unable to let this go, to get over it, why was she so stuck in my head. I came across all manner of answers. Was she a narcissist? A psychopath? BPD? BPD fit the bill to some extent, and for a while that kind of made sense. Relationships with those with BPD can indeed be devastating, there were certainly some of the signs. It made some sense, and this is what I ran with, and it made sense of things for a while.

It wasn't like a regular heartbreak, it was nothing like when Karen and I had split. It had taken a few months of feeling a bit crap but life goes on, we can't hold onto things that no longer serve us. It's like an energy that surrounds you, like being chased by a swarm of angry wasps. You just want to scream "FUCK OFF" I didn't want Sarah to just turn up, that would have fixed absolutely nothing. I was left with this hanging around me like a lead weight.

At the end of the summer, I decided to give up the house I was renting. I hardly needed it to be honest, I needed everything to focus on building the new business. I moved into the warehouse office. Quite frankly I don't mind. I'm a boy scout and I can sleep anywhere.

As Christmas rolled in things really did seem to be picking up again, I was on top of my cocaine habit, we were all enjoying each other's company and work was fun again. Things had started to calm down with regards to Sarah, which was a relief. And just when things started to go well, my world would be turned upside down.

Everything Is an Illusion, Just A Very Persistent One

I was casually browsing YouTube, watching random clips, when I stumbled upon something called the Mandela Effect. I had heard of it before – it's this idea that people remember things incorrectly. I was about to skip the video when I noticed JFK's car in the thumbnail. Now, I haven't mentioned it, but I love a good mystery, and JFK's assassination is certainly one of life's great mysteries. And yes, I can tell you all about who shot whom, when, and how. No, Lee Harvey Oswald did not fire a shot that day. I can even tell you about the umbrella man who claimed in court that he was protesting Clement Attlee when he was actually signalling for more bullets. I can tell you the Zapruder film was tampered with to hide the fact that William Greer, the Irish American driver with a drinking problem, stopped the car on the signal of a Cuban man who stepped into the road waving his fist. I can even tell you about the CIA pilot who flew Charles Nicoletti in, one of the Mafia shooters from the Dal-Tex building. Officer Tippets wash shot by Roscoe White of the Dallas PD and Gary Marlow

So, armed with this knowledge, I decided to watch the clip, curious to see what people misremembered. What people didn't remember was that there were six people in the car and what the divider was doing there. And shockingly, I was one of those people. I was in utter disbelief – I literally fell off my chair. I knew there were four people in the car, not thought, knew. I clearly recalled that Mrs Connelly was in LBJ's car. I even remembered Governor Connelly being interviewed, expressing his last thoughts about his wife, wondering if he'd ever see her again and if she was okay. Well, now she was sitting right next to him, and that interview doesn't seem to exist either.

The next one was Queens "We are the champions", a song I'd listened to many times on my Walkman on my paper round. Before I phones we had tapes, and so often we listened to the same tape over and over. We are the champions, does not finish with "of the world"?? Well, it certainly did all the times I'd listened to it. This was insane, like what the hell?

I was in a daze, was this some sort of internet trick? What the hell was this world? Do we live in the matrix after all? Am I in the Truman show? This was the strangest thing I've ever experienced, and yes I've seen ghosts (a curious common experience with twin flames)

I was determined to find an explanation because things don't just change, right? So, I started searching for answers and stumbled upon Reddit posts about the Mandela Effect. This only made things even weirder. Mickey Mouse no longer had his braces, the Monopoly Man no longer had a monocle, and then there was the A-Team van. It was no longer black with a red stripe; it now had a grey top. But I knew for a fact that the A-Team van was all black with a red stripe. I had organised crazy rallies across Europe where people would show up in cars dressed up like the A-Team, and all those vans were black with a red stripe. Uncle Sam no longer had a red striped hat.

I messaged Bill, the guy I had set up the rallies with, and I knew exactly what he would say: "Don't be daft." He sent me an A-Team clip, and there it was – the black van with the red stripe. I showed it to the chef who was working for me at the time, and we both agreed that we remembered the A-Team van as black with a red stripe. We looked at each other, relieved, thinking this must be some kind of internet hoax or a psy-op to drive us crazy.

The quest for a rational explanation continued. Three days after I had watched the A-Team van clip with my chef, another friend named Kieran paid me a visit. I decided to ask him about the A-Team van, fully expecting him to confirm that it was black with a red stripe, as he had always been a big fan of the show. He was absolutely certain it was black with a red stripe, 100% sure. To support my case, I showed him a couple of photos from the internet featuring the A-Team van with the grey top, and he immediately dismissed them as mock-ups, agreeing with my assessment.

Then, I showed him the clip with the red van, the one that we had watched a few days earlier. I confidently played the clip for him, saying, "This is the one you recall." But what happened next completely blew our minds. The same clip we had watched just three days prior had changed. The van was now black with a red stripe and a grey top. It was the same clip, the same link, but the van had changed before our eyes.

The chef and I exchanged bewildered glances, while Kieran, growing increasingly loud, insisted that this was just some kind of internet trick and attempted to dismiss it as quickly as possible. However, for us, there was no dismissing it. We had both seen the change, and there was no way we could have remembered it incorrectly. I was left utterly dumbfounded by this inexplicable phenomenon.

The Chef was equally bemused at the soviet flag now having a star. He had spent his childhood under soviet rule. It was the first he had ever seen of that.

He had a sleepless night that night.

As my fascination and obsession with the Mandela Effect grew, I couldn't help but see the world in a new light. It felt like I was witnessing a hint of magic, coupled with profound astonishment. The more I delved into this phenomenon, the more astonishing changes I discovered. The Earth had shifted within the Milky Way, relocating from the Sagittarius arm to the Orion spur. The sun had changed colour, from yellow to white, Australia's position in the ocean had shifted, Easter Island had been discovered inhabited now and always had been, and the moon now exhibited a Cheshire Cat phase.

All of this led me to the belief that we might actually be living in a matrix-like reality. This perspective was amplified by my previous experience of hearing a voice, which I truly believed to be the voice of God, on the day Sarah had disappeared from my life.

Though I haven't mentioned it, I had another encounter with our creator a few months back, this is personal to me. But let's say he has a sense of humour. All this thee, thou, fe fi fo fum nonsense seems contrived human grandiosity, compared with my experience of a lighthearted, fun and most importantly, loving God.

Amidst this spiritual upheaval, I crossed paths with Sofia, an Estonian woman who owned her own cleaning business and serviced our office. She was an attractive redhead with a no-nonsense attitude, and her business seemed to be doing well.

Dating Sofia brought a sense of normalcy back into my life. She was considerate, paid for outings, and seemed genuinely interested in making me happy. It was a refreshing change from the previous tumultuous years where I felt like I was shouldering all the emotional labor. Watching Game of Thrones together allowed us to enjoy simple moments of normalcy, curling up on the sofa without the drama that had plagued my recent past.

The gradual disappearance of friends from my life became evident as my status changed. No longer the prominent business owner I once was, people seemed to keep their distance. Some who had claimed to be loyal friends simply stopped communicating with me. I experienced a sense of relief with some of these departures, particularly in the case of Karen. She had stuck around for as long as it suited her, but as our circumstances changed, our communication dwindled, and I found myself indifferent to her absence.

Sofia was only 10 years my junior, so a marked improvement. But in other ways she was far more sensible and grounded than I was. The loose entrepreneur Del Boy type character.

All this time Angela worked with me, she had been working for me for ten years and she was a rock to be around. We started to really get on well, she was now happily married, I was in a relationship, the business was doing OK and life again seemed to be starting to feel almost normal again.

But alas it was not to last, after a few months I simply could not find it in me to take the relationship with Sofia any further, it just seemed to stop within me, my feelings defying my own logic. There wasn't anything wrong, it's just that something within me kind of gave up, stopped, the energy just wasn't there. I wasn't comparing her, nor was I thinking much of Sarah at this point.

The VOID

My ego had continued to crumble, I noticed every time I tried to force things, such as the business, it would simply push back, like when you're trying to run in a dream but just can't. I found myself pondering the deeper meaning of all that had transpired. I had an inexplicable sense that everything was somehow destined.

As I reflected, it became clear that my former identity had been tied to the big business I once owned – the car I drove, the places I frequented – and I had lost sight of who I truly was. Being a boss had thrust me into roles and situations that most people would rather avoid – delivering difficult news, meting out discipline, and maintaining an air of authority to ensure that everyone did their job. Being big and scary didn't seem to fit with what I truly felt inside.

A part of me was aware that my old maverick persona, the daring adventurer, was slowly fading away. It was like a part of me was dying along with the loss of my former life. I had lost everything, and I felt like a nobody. The dreams of building a family and achieving great success had been shattered, leaving me with a sense of hopelessness and resignation. What was the point of it all?

The business continued to trudge along, but it was just that – okay. Every effort to push it forward seemed to result in just enough business to cover the expenses we incurred. Conversely, when we tried to cut back, we would lose business, nullifying any potential savings. Even Angela, my colleague, noticed that something seemed very strange about our situation. It was as if we were being kept afloat by some mysterious force. No matter what we did, nothing seemed to work, and we were constantly teetering on the edge.

Losing the rented offices and warehouse space was another blow, as the landlord went back on his word. It seemed like betrayal was par for the course. With no physical space left for the business, I had to find a new place to call home.

In February 2018 I had found myself homeless at times, even sleeping in my car on occasion. Andy, a former employee and now a friend, kindly allowed me to stay at his place during this challenging period. It was a humbling experience for someone who had once been a successful business owner.

An old adversary turned friend, a fellow entrepreneur, eloquently expressed our shared reality. "We are entrepreneurs," he stated, "we sleep in our cars and in our mansions." His words resonated with me. It might not be the ideal situation, but I've come to embrace every aspect of my journey, because, ultimately, I'm accountable for everything that transpires in my life. I never adopted a victim mentality throughout this. After all, when climbing a mountain, one must anticipate a few stumbles along the way. I've developed a certain resilience, and a few chilly nights in my car aren't enough to faze a seasoned individual like me. That's Sarah's purpose on this planet.

In the midst of this turmoil, I made a decision that had been a long-time dream of mine. I decided to buy a boat. The idea of living on a boat had always appealed to me, and at this point in my life, being a single guy with no family to provide for, it seemed like the perfect time to pursue this dream. I was in my mid-forties, deep in debt, but the idea of a different kind of lifestyle was calling to me.

I found myself caring less and less about conforming to the expectations of the world I had known, which I now began to suspect wasn't the ultimate reality. Though I still wasn't fully aware of what lay beyond, I was becoming increasingly convinced that there was more to life than what met the eye.

And this was the VOID, that space in between the dissolution of the ego and a spiritual awakening. Though at the time I wasn't sure about ever reaching the point where I'd feel in any way grounded again. I found it increasingly difficult to relate to society as

I once did. It had become clear to me that nothing we perceive is truly real, and I could write an entire book on that subject. I discovered solace among like-minded individuals on Reddit, and it was heartening to see even Elon Musk delving into these discussions. When Elon suggests there's a 1 in 17 million chance (an arbitrary figure, it seems) that we're living in base reality, it becomes headline news, and what a brilliant mind he is. Yet when someone like me conveys a similar message, it often gets dismissed as eccentric ramblings: "Don't pay attention to the peculiar man, children."

I can't say that life was good or bad, it was just meh. I can't say I was an addict or clean during that time. My addiction, like it used to be, certainly had departed. But I still used cocaine as my escape from the drudgery of the void.

Occasionally, Andy would visit the boat, and we both seemed to share a sense of living out our days in a rather lackluster manner, just plodding along. It felt like we had reached the end, a tale of trying and failing. Andy brought me news that Sarah had landed a high-flying job, and it almost seemed as though our energies had somehow intertwined. Deep inside, I still sensed her presence, and it was as if a part of her had found its way into me, and vice versa. After all, I was the one known for my drive, tenacity, and bravado, not the one simply trudging through life's motions. This used to be Sarah's role.

Not a day went by without Sarah crossing my mind, though often it was merely as background noise – an occasional fleeting thought that I could easily dismiss. This pattern persisted throughout 2018 and into 2019. My emotions would fluctuate, yet for the most part, I managed to carry on with the business of life.

Throughout this time, I would still pray, knowing now there was more to this world and this life that we know. I still resented the fact that I had worked so hard to get where I was, and here I was struggling against debt again. I felt very alone most of the time, but still somehow, I kept some faith that this was my path. I didn't understand it, but I accepted it.

Every now and then I would find myself battling the blues, using cocaine to mask the situation, only to exacerbate it of course. I briefly went back to the anonymous meetings, only to find I didn't fit in there anymore. I felt my connection with God was stronger than most of those preaching about it. And indeed, it was, if it wasn't for that connection, I'm not sure how I would have carried on. The void is a tough place to be, and it can last years.

LOCKDOWN

I was well aware of the unfolding situation long before the lockdown measures were officially declared. Contacts within my industry had already informed me of preparations being made as early as February, even before the pandemic was formally announced. I saw it as the setup it was. When the lockdown was finally imposed, we lost all prospects of future business, leaving us with no option but to close up shop.

Here was yet another business endeavour coming to a close, this time without all the dramatic twists and turns. Nonetheless, it presented me with an opportunity to explore something new. I considered it another solution to my challenges, a chance to immerse myself in a different venture and regain my focus on the future.

At that juncture, Angela and I were the sole remaining members of the team, and I was genuinely grateful to have her by my side. Our bond had grown strong, and our collaborative efforts had proven successful, especially when dealing with major clients. Disagreements were a rare occurrence, and our communication was generally smooth.

With this camaraderie, we embarked on our new venture, and things initially appeared promising. I had developed a remarkable product that performed well, and sales were robust at the outset.

The future once again held a glimmer of hope, but regrettably, it was short-lived, about two weeks short lived. External factors beyond our control disrupted our marketing plans, as Google's commitment to privacy posed significant challenges.

Still, I had learnt that it takes courage and determination to make things work. And so, I again soldiered on, briefly getting some breaks, only for them to fall short again. Then came Brexit and the supply chain went to pot for us. Without going into incessant detail, small companies like us were shelved by the distributors to make way for their big suppliers who had lost European business.

We persevered with this endeavour for about a year. Angela, who was expecting her second child, had to step back, leaving just me to manage the operations intermittently, with Andy helping out during lockdown. In truth, I had a sense that this venture would struggle to get off the ground. Buoyed up though by positive reviews. Nevertheless, I had already departed from my previous industry, and moving forward was the only path ahead.

It was April when Angela's Father died, her mother slipping into a coma that same day. She was three weeks from giving birth. My thoughts were with her during this awful time.

The Awakening

This was the setting for a significant revelation, or perhaps I should say, rude awakening. Up until this point, I had acknowledged the existence of a creator, but it was something I had taken in my stride, while going about the business of living as normal life as possible.

Sarah, however, continued to enter my thoughts briefly on most days. The emotions tied to these thoughts varied, at times pleasant, and at others, tinged with anger, mostly directed at myself for what I considered my foolishness. I was still without answers as to why I couldn't shake these feelings completely or why I hadn't managed to "move on" as people often reminded me.

It was exactly 5 years to the day that on that fateful morning when I heard God's voice, when Sarah had gone. Mick, a long-term contractor came to see me. We didn't see each other much at all, we had a working relationship. He was a freelancer in my old industry, but like many, lockdown had taken his business. He came to me for advice as to how to wind his company down.

Coincidentally, as he was in the process of deactivating his Instagram account, he stumbled upon a picture of Sarah. He didn't follow her, and she didn't follow him. His suspicion was that the image had come into his view because someone who followed him on the platform also followed her – an old employee of mine.

He commented that she was looking good. In the post, Andy had occasionally shown me pictures from her Facebook, as they were still friends on that platform. To be honest, it hadn't had much of an impact on me, and I certainly wasn't the type to engage in social media stalking – that just struck me as creepy.

Before I said anything either way, he had got his phone up and showed me her photo. She was indeed looking great, and here was I, in a mess with this new venture.

I have no idea why, but this set something off in me. Energy started running about my body, independent of any thought, it was like I was being electrically charged. I tried shaking it off and tried focusing on something else. I started getting frustrated with myself, frustrated and angry at her, this started a loop in my head until I was plain furious, you know the type of anger where you start cursing at yourself out loud?

I thought back to that day I prayed for her, how I knew that my life was going to tank, I scolded myself at being so silly, why had I done that for someone that simply didn't care one bit about me?

As I walked back to my boat, preoccupied with my thoughts, just hoping this would pass. I again heard that voice.

"Do you regret it"?

Like it was listening to my thoughts, in fact, it was indeed listening to my thoughts

This is hard to explain, but it's not like when a human being asks you something, your instant emotional answer easy to give, this is God, you can't lie, it's not that you may not want to, you can't, everything is laid bare.

Inside the answer was obvious to me

"No"

I don't regret it at all, and I didn't know why.

With that response, something occurred that I struggle to convey adequately. It felt like a vortex had opened up within me, a swirling chasm from another dimension, something immense. A part of me had been unlocked, and that's the only way I can describe it. Some call it the opening of a heart chakra. I guess that would be an explanation.

I was left feeling dizzy, confused, and in a genuine state of wonder. What had just transpired? Yet, this time, it was accompanied by a sense of fascination. I was transported back to those days after Sarah's departure when I couldn't sleep, and she occupied the forefront of my thoughts. Would this ever come to an end?

I found myself completely consumed by thoughts of Sarah. Was this some form of karma I needed to resolve, or a life lesson I had yet to address? What was happening to me? It had been five years since she left, and it felt as fresh as if it were just yesterday.

Despite my efforts to carry on with life, I began to notice an unusual abundance of feathers wherever I went. Living on a boat, some feathers might be expected, but this was different. Feathers appeared during my runs, even swimming in the sea a great big white feather would be floating in front of me, and even during countryside walks meant to distract me from these thoughts.

I confided in an open-minded female friend about this strange phenomenon, and as we walked and talked, feathers appeared where I was walking, yet none in front of her. It was nothing short of bewildering.

I was totally consumed, I didn't know what to do, I was losing my damn mind. I started google searching, and it was then I stumbled across the concept of twin flames. Strange, I had never heard of this before, maybe I wasn't massively spiritual, but still I read tarot every now and then so you'd expect this to be something I should have heard of. Especially since I'd already done some searching a few years prior on this.

And so I read (please note this is what is on the internet, but it has been my experience, I'm not sure this list is definitive, it's what was put in front of me at the time, fate wanted me to see this)

Your twin flame is there to invoke a spiritual awakening ? Check yes
You may have a birthday in common with one of their close family members? Check yes, mine and her sisters the same day
Never quite being girlfriend or boyfriend
Lots of triggering
One generally runs.
One is more spiritual.
Large age gap
1111 plays a part in the connection.
Birthdays are significant

And so on

"Holy fuck"!! I was left astounded, finally something made sense, finally an answer that I wasn't going completely nuts, this was what I was being pushed to see. I could sense spirit/god/universe showing me this, my sense of relief palpable. At last, some sort of an answer as to why I couldn't shake this.

I started delving more and more, and every turn just kept on solidifying what I was finding out. This is insane, my eternal partner was Sarah. Well that explains why I always felt the way I did for sure, the magnetism between us was incredibly strong.

But how could this be? It felt utterly insane. I admonished myself to regain control, to dismiss it as mere wishful thinking. Why would I wish for someone to be my eternal partner when it appeared that they didn't care in the least about me? My mind was a whirlwind of confusing thoughts and questions, all racing through my head.

This turmoil of confusion and thoughts wouldn't release its grip on me. I could hardly concentrate on anything else; even simple tasks like shopping felt like a burden. I'd find myself picking items from the shelves, but my mind was consumed by these thoughts, as if a swarm of angry wasps buzzed around me. I swayed from denial to instincts, to logic, and somewhere in between, unsure of where to anchor my thoughts and emotions. How can one person have this hold on me?

Sarah was a constant presence in my mind, from the very moment I woke up, even before I opened my eyes, to the instant I fell asleep. There was not a single second that passed without her being there, not as thoughts, but as an ever-present presence.

I needed a break; I just couldn't take it anymore. So, like any grown man facing a life-shattering experience, I did what most would do and went to my mother's. During the drive up there, I could vividly envision Sarah with stars falling all around her. I could see her gazing up in awe at the beauty of the glittering stars, and I could sense her happiness. This, in turn, brought me joy. My emotions swung back and forth on that drive, oscillating between an overwhelming sense of love and overpowering fear, almost like a trance that I had to snap out of periodically. It was an intense and confusing mix of emotions.

My visit to Mum's place was a much-needed break. I was utterly exhausted and felt completely worn down. She lived near a beach, and I made it a daily ritual to walk down to the shore and meditate. It helped take the edge off the chaos I had been experiencing. Finally, after three weeks of what felt like sheer madness, I started to regain some semblance of sanity.

During this time, I picked up "A Course in Miracles," a book mum had tried to read but had mostly found challenging to understand. To my surprise, I found myself comprehending much more than I had initially expected. It made me reflect on how far I had come spiritually in just five years.

Signs

Whilst on a walk in a local beauty spot with my mother, the abundance of feathers persisted. However, it was during these walks that I began to notice something unusual – pigeons appearing to cross my path almost on cue. This might not sound that strange, and indeed I initially dismissed it, but it felt like they were responding to my thoughts. In my mind, I'd think, "Fly across," and one of them would indeed do so. I couldn't help but feel like I was losing my mind, and with that thought, a pigeon would swoop down towards me, reinforcing my sense of insanity.

Even when I was 400 miles away from home, I couldn't escape this overwhelming experience. A change of scenery didn't offer any respite. The only solace I found was through meditation, so I turned to it more frequently. It became my lifeline, my only escape from this chaotic situation.

On the drive back, my attention was drawn to license plates. It seemed like everywhere I looked, there were combinations like 69, 444, 111, and 222. It was as if no one had ordinary plates anymore. The number 69 appeared repeatedly, and I assumed it must have been a popular year for car registrations. It all felt overwhelming. To soothe my soul, I listened to Viking healing music throughout the entire journey, grasping at anything that could bring me some peace.

I'm almost home and I can see my boat bobbing away. "OK, I'm tough" I say to myself "pull yourself out of this, no more twin flame nonsense, get yourself together" My head down, I felt a new sense of determination.

It was then I looked up from the steering wheel, and in lights, right on front of me 1111

The taxi company the numbers belonged to was a local one apparently, one I've never seen in 20 years of living here, and one I have never seen again.

I was beaten, my two seconds worth of determination gone.

And 1111 is the twin flame number, and yes, we see it, all the time. I looked into significant dates. Our first kiss 26 11:11 or 8 11:11 (infinity 11:11). Our birthdays are 6 months and 9 days apart. (69 is yin yang, the feminine masculine energies) Numerology surrounds twins. None of us really know why, maybe just to run our damn stubborn faces in it when we want to deny this connection is real. But it certainly confirmed what I was already sensing inside. I saw 11:11 on the clock every day, 11:11 on you tube 11 comments, 11 upvotes and so on.

That she was me, and I was her. We were one, the same. The exact same, the only other soul in the universe that was the exact same as me. And it did make sense, in a didn't make sense kind of way, we both sensed that something was different. I always said we were the exact same inside, totally different on the surface.

Yet knowing this seemed to bring more pain. And a yearning.

I dropped to my knees, begging to be released from this hell, only God could help now. I was out of any other options. My own self-determination was worth nothing. Nothing seems to work. I could feel Sarah's energy all around me now, it was so strong that it was like she was next to me. I could hear her voice, smell her and yes, even talk to her. It wasn't "like" she was with me. She was with me. It wasn't an imagined thing; it was very real.

I would talk to her in the car, out loud conversations. And even arguments. I truly felt as if I was losing my mind.

All I could do was resort to prayer, running, exercise and meditation, whatever it took to get me through the day. Occasionally, I'd turn to drinking and even cocaine in an attempt to numb the overwhelming sense of Sarah's presence. While on some level it felt comforting to have her around in this way, it also resurfaced old wounds, causing anger to well up within me. Our last parting had hit me particularly hard, and I didn't ask for much from people, but being treated as if I were worthless was one of those things I couldn't tolerate. Call me mr picky.

I'd ask the universe for signs, and without delay, they would manifest. One of these signs was especially intriguing. I was riding my bike along my regular route, beseeching the cosmos for some confirmation that what I was experiencing was real. Instantly, about 200 meters ahead of me, a flock of pigeons descended, roughly 50 of them, and within that group, there were two white doves. As I approached, the other pigeons dispersed, but the two white doves stayed till I was nearly on top of them, they took flight, fluttered up into the air, and soared alongside me. It was also the feeling that accompanied this, it was serene, it felt like this was just for me. It's a strange feeling seeing nature perform a dance just for your benefit, it kind of makes you feel a little special. Though why I needed to know this I just didn't understand.

These signs were not subtle by any means. I'd ask for a bird of prey to fly above, and one would appear, it was as if the simulated universe was built for me alone and was showing off. It was astounding, mesmerising and just something I couldn't share with a single soul. This may sound small, but it was countless times this would happen. One or two could easily be explained away.

Gradually, with more and more meditation, the overwhelming sense of her presence began to diminish once again. It had been two months, and it was now July. But it felt like two years since this all began, which was back in May. I met an old friend at the pub. He wasn't particularly inclined toward spirituality, but his wife certainly was. Still feeling the effects of the spiritual turmoil I had been experiencing, I shared my story with him. When he asked to see a picture of her, I hesitated but ultimately showed him her Instagram profile. His immediate dismissal seemed to suggest he thought I was merely infatuated with her looks, given how attractive she appeared in the photo.

Who knows, maybe that was it. I was clinging to any possibility to make sense of this twin flames concept, the idea of an eternal partner. How could this be? Why? What was happening? Maybe I was just a horny old dog, maybe I really was that shallow. I went to the toilet, washed my hands, and looked at myself in the large mirror, giving myself that "really?" Look. Then something extraordinary began to occur. My eyes started to change; they took on the hue and sparkle of her eyes. The colour transformed, and her sparkle was reflected in mine.

Returning to the pub table, I asked my friend, "Do my eyes look different?" I needed reassurance to determine if what I was experiencing was real or just in my head. He replied, "Yes" He said curiously "they're sparkling."

I couldn't hold on any longer. I had to make my excuses. I made my way back to the boat, head down. As soon as I was in I dropped to my knees and cried like a baby. Everything just came flooding out, the love I had for Sarah, the pain of it all as well, I had completely given in, I had to accept this or I was done. That was my only choice left, no fighting it. No going back and forward, no dismissing it. I was in the hands of God, only this time I had to mean it. I just couldn't go on like this any more. It was like trying to contain a force bursting out of every pore. Every second of the day.

The Lessons Begin

The very next day I met with Angela, it was a beautiful July morning and we had a coffee. It was the first time I'd seen her since March, just before her father had passed. It was really good to see her. As I expected she said she couldn't continue with the business any more. Of course I understood. Quite frankly I had all but given up with the business, only doing something because I didn't know what else to do.

I told her about what had been happening with Sarah. Angela being less than impressed with Sarah's behaviour when she left the company, thought me crazy of course. It had been Angela who had been by my side for years. In fact we shared a far better relationship than Sarah and I. Sarah would avoid any type of grown-up conversation, happier to create discord than harmony. Whereas Angela was straight talking and honest. Yes, I liked Angela as a person far more. But that's not how twin flames work.

As one era ended another immediately began. And that was of my ascension. I already knew there was a creator, I knew reincarnation was a thing, I knew the universe was a simulated reality created by source/ god/ the universe of which we are a part.

I would have vivid dreams about Sarah. Like a series of dreams where we would gradually start talking to one another again. I don't normally recall dreams but those I did.

Every day there was a download, a lesson from the cosmos, something during the day would happen and I would be asked by spirit what I had learnt. It may have been a curt cashier to whom another time I would have been equally as rude back.

The recurring question that arose was, "What have I learned?" For instance, when someone cut me off in traffic, I began to consider that they might be having a rough day, facing job dissatisfaction, or dealing with family problems. In essence, I was being guided to think beyond my immediate reactions and to empathise with the struggles of others. This is just one example, and while it may seem obvious, putting it into practice is far more challenging than it sounds.

It genuinely felt like I was attending a daily class of life. Each day, something would occur, often seemingly trivial incidents. A person would smile, I would lose some money, or something would transpire, and the universe would gently nudge me, signalling that I had a lesson to absorb. Occasionally, it required some contemplation to grasp the significance of what I was being shown. Frequently, these lessons seemed so evident and pertained to what we might consider minor events, but I now understand that it's often the small things that hold the key to making a profound difference.

What was less obvious, even more of my ego was being stripped away bit by bit. And I was being taught to trust in the universe.

But with that I was able to see others' egos. The suit of armour people constantly walked around with. I saw others' pain and struggles, sometimes an overly strutting guy would walk past. Trying to look tough, yet all I could see was fear. It was quite amusing at times. Though I'll be honest I didn't judge anyone. After all I recognised my own failings whilst walking around carrying the weight of a big ego.

Some of the lessons I encountered were far from trivial. I was confronted with the memories of my father's behaviour, an alcoholic of the worst kind, who subjected me to physical, emotional, and mental bullying. He was quick to criticise and bully, sparing compliments. He had an unrelenting need for control, disregarding others' feelings about things, and yet, he was also quick to retreat at the first sign of difficulty. I despised him, to the point where even at his funeral, I couldn't find a single positive thing to say. I was 26 when he passed away, and I had to shoulder the responsibility of handling the funeral arrangements, clearing out his apartment, and more.

For most of my life, I believed I was stronger than to be deeply affected by someone so evidently selfish and arrogant. After all, I had moved out of my home when I was just 16, and while it had been a bumpy road, I had managed quite well. But what became glaringly obvious was that I hadn't truly forgiven him. When faced with his spirit, which I could clearly sense, I finally forgave him. I understood that, despite his behaviour, he was only doing his best, just like anyone else, to navigate through life, to find meaning and purpose, all while being scared and feeling utterly alone.

It's difficult to put into words what that period was like, but everything else in life appeared inconsequential, trivial, and unrelated to the profound lessons I was gaining. Many of these lessons were things I had believed I understood, and in some sense, I did intellectually, but I hadn't truly incorporated them into my life. I wasn't very forgiving; I often responded with anger or retaliation. It felt as though I was being led through a rigorous spiritual education.

My feelings for Sarah would vary wildly from love to outright hatred, spilling over to self hatred, sometimes even to the point I needed to fall back on old ways to calm the energy. Sitting cross legged going ohm doesn't always work out quite as well as some yogi may suggest.

Throughout this time though, as I continued to meditate, Sarah remained a constant presence in my thoughts every day. The concept of the twin flame connection remained a prominent aspect of my evolving self. However, I was still struggling to fully grasp its significance, and from time to time, I questioned my own sanity. It was the persistent nudges from the universe that served as a constant reminder that what I was experiencing was far from ordinary but, in some inexplicable way, part of a natural process.

The other venture had ended in failure, and I had invested a significant amount of money into it. It left me pondering what the purpose of it all had been. Time and again, glimmers of hope would emerge, only to fade away. Despite the valuable lessons I was gaining from the experience, I couldn't comprehend what had driven me to embark on this journey. I had created a highly effective weight loss product that received positive feedback and produced results, yet it didn't succeed. Little did I know at the time that this too would be a piece of the puzzle I would come to comprehend later on.

Throughout this journey, friends gradually faded away, some of whom I had known for decades. It was a two-way street – either I chose to sever ties when they were needlessly unpleasant, or they simply distanced themselves from me. Among them were individuals I had actively supported, both emotionally and financially, having provided substantial business opportunities and assistance during their times of need. In many cases, it felt as though I had been guided to help them. The departure of some was a source of sadness. This process had been ongoing for the past five years, but during 2020 to 2022, it seemed to intensify. I was starting to experience a heightened sense of solitude and a growing sense of being drawn closer to a higher power.

Move Into An RV

It was then a clear message came to sell the boat, I had been living in the marina 4 years now, and to be honest it was quite peaceful. The gym on my doorstep, people I knew when I wanted to go to the pub, it really wasn't that bad if a little insular.

As has often been the case in the past few years, life's events unfolded in ways that brought me to my knees once more, with only a few options left to explore. I had walked away from my previous profession and had no desire to return, and the alternative venture didn't pan out. However, my artistic talents were flourishing, and I had developed a newfound passion for art. Surprisingly, others appreciated my work as well. Unbeknownst to me, this is a common experience for twins; we often discover a creative outlet, such as writing, poetry, art, or music. I had authored a book, begun learning to play the guitar, and was now successfully selling my artwork. I felt distinctly different from most people at the moment, yet ironically, I found myself embodying a walking stereotype of that of the Twin Flame.

I found myself doing things I had previously been averse to, such as working for someone else. Surprisingly, I discovered that I actually enjoyed it. Although it wasn't a long-term arrangement, the lessons were clear and relentless, chipping away at any remnants of ego or notions of superiority I might have harboured. It taught me the value of humility and the idea that no task should be considered beneath me.

The following months were a bit chaotic. I had my van, which had some value, and my plan was simply to wander and let life unfold. I found myself parking on the side of the road on several occasions, even facing the challenge of contracting COVID and enduring cold nights in the back of the van, nestled next to a golf course.

Finding myself back at one of my former storage locations that I had used for my previous business, I just happened to pop by. As fate would have it, they were in need of someone to stay on-site, and as a stroke of luck, they had a small barn where I could pursue my art. When you're in tune with the spirit and follow its guidance, coincidences tend to hold fewer surprises. In alignment with this flow, I decided to sell my van and invest in an RV.

So here I was in solitude, a couple of remaining friends to talk to, even Andy had moved away and stopped talking to me, like so many others. Some seemingly out of the blue for absolutely no reason. As is the way when we start to awaken.

I discovered that I required less meditation, and I connected with fellow twins, the internet had its merits in facilitating these connections. My own experiences served to assist others, and in return, their insights helped me make sense of the tumultuous journey I had been on. While I had felt utterly isolated, I realised that there were others navigating similar paths. For instance, a corporate lawyer from New York had left her job to pursue psychology in a quest to understand the profound changes in her life. Happily married women found themselves meeting their twins, who were two decades their junior. There were also individuals discussing the challenging prospect of ending it all. Many of us would describe this journey as bittersweet.

For many of us, including myself, our previous lives lie in ruins all around us, with nothing remaining of the past, not even our egos and the identities we once clung to. Our dreams and ambitions have also dissipated. We find ourselves surrendered to a higher power, and despite our relentless struggles, we have no other option. This is what it means to be in the service of a divine force. Whether we actively sought it or not, there was a part of me that sensed this was the soul's chosen path.

Never Say Never Again

Life began to settle down once more, and while my art wasn't soaring to new heights, I did manage to sell a few paintings and receive numerous compliments, which was gratifying. However, smiles alone couldn't pay the bills, and I inevitably found myself being drawn back to my former business – the one I had firmly declared I was finished with. It's a curious thing how as soon as I decide something won't happen, it has a knack for proving me wrong. Despite a divine and all-knowing God who is the creator of all, and me with my... i phone. I must admit that at times, I did go kicking and screaming in some directions.

Throughout this journey, the intense energy I had been experiencing gradually waned. Sarah continued to occupy my thoughts daily, though not constantly, the best way I can describe it is like working in an office with a pink wall, it never really goes away but you get used to it, and eventually kind of ignore it. I had managed to forgive those I believed had wronged me in my life, and I had developed a newfound compassion for the trials and tribulations faced by my fellow humans on this challenging mission called life.

The final forgiveness was directed inward, towards both myself and Sarah, recognising that we were essentially one and the same as twin souls. By this point, I had come to understand that whatever had unfolded in our journey was precisely what we had intended on a soul level. It felt destined, as if events had occurred beyond my control – even supernatural experiences that I had never imagined I'd encounter.

In forgiving myself for behaviours that seemed beyond my usual control, I also considered that, in the context of a twin flame connection, it was only fair to assume that this forgiveness worked both ways. This connection is a complex and transformative one and forgiving ourselves and each other is a pivotal step in the healing and growth process.

Often, we are left confused, we meet the person we love more than life itself, and then they reject us and bolt. It's confusing, in some cases twins don't even have any kind of relationship, they can be brief meetings. Like me, many of us are activated and shown the connection years after they have met. Scrambling for answers for what is going on. None of us had heard of twin flames before, since we resided in a dimension where they just didn't seem to exist.

This was clear to me since I had searched tirelessly for answers after Sarah bolted, there's no way I wouldn't have come across twin flames in that search. One I seemed to have found so easily when I was activated 5 years later.

After seven long years of being led by the spirit, through challenging, disheartening, and tumultuous times, enduring constant loss and trials, I had reached a place of peace. I had developed a deep trust in God, believing that everything would ultimately be fine. At last, I had surrendered to the divine plan.

Trusting in a Divine creator despite the carnage may indeed seem strange at first. It may appear as though the universe is less than loving during these periods of intense growth. However, it's crucial to recognise that the "beating" isn't aimed at our core selves but rather at the ego and the constructs of our self-identity that no longer serve a purpose.

I have no plans, no ambitions, the fast living confident prideful person I once was has dissipated, in a sense we die a death whilst alive, to find our soul's purpose. Often that purpose is just to be, as healing ourselves and awakening has huge ramifications of the energy of the planet. This may be a bit much to go into at this time. But for those that understand such matters or have had an near death experience this may make some sense.

When we come to a profound understanding that we are souls inhabiting human bodies, rather than just human bodies with a soul, we start to grasp the significance of these trials and tribulations. They are the necessary tools for our spiritual evolution, guiding us toward the state of being we are meant to reach. The journey, though challenging, serves a higher purpose in aligning us with our true essence.

Peace

In my experience, when you truly find inner peace, the intensity of the connection with your twin flame diminishes. The obsessions, dreams, and constant thoughts tend to subside. However, this doesn't necessarily mean that the connection with your twin flame ceases to exist. In fact, quite the opposite. It's precisely what your twin flame is meant to do – to help you learn these challenging life lessons. After all they are you in many senses, and they have to ascend with you, there is no choice, whilst it may not look anything like you're doing this together, you are in fact a team. But the trick is, only one of you is aware of the connection. Well at least at the start anyway.

The ultimate lesson is to be at peace with ourselves, to find a sense of completeness without needing external factors to fill the void. Look around at the world, and you'll see many people who would crumble if they lost their homes, jobs, or spouses. Yet, for many of us who have walked the path of the twin flame, we've faced the loss of nearly everything we once fought for. We find ourselves on the fringes of society, inhabiting the cold, harsh edges. And yet, in that very experience, we are achieving by simply enduring and evolving through it.

It's true that those who embark on a spiritual journey, especially a twin flame journey, often find themselves in a lonely space. Conversations about these profound experiences can be met with raised eyebrows or, in the worst cases, skepticism. It's challenging for others to grasp the depth of these experiences if they haven't walked a similar path. And yes, we do view the world through a different lens, seeing ego, fear, and false pride from a perspective that, in retrospect, can seem rather comical.

Synchronicities are a common thread in this journey. Many times, we feel almost compelled to do things, as if guided by a force beyond our control. I hadn't previously paid attention to numerology or signs, I found myself surrounded by numbers and symbols that take on a new significance in the context of this spiritual journey – 1717, 1616, 1111, 69, and so on. I still see these numbers, they serve more as a guide that I'm on the right path, that spirit is still there, watching over me.

The Lessons and Where This Leads Us

I wasn't sure whether to include every spiritual aspect of what I learnt and when along the road, to be honest I think that may have broken things up too much and been hard to follow. At the time of writing this book it's been 3 years since I was shown I was a twin, 8 years since I even saw Sarah. 13 years since we first met, this is no short-term thing.

For the most part it had been a gruelling, miserable and at times an insane few years. Materially successful it had not been, that's for sure. Though it was also wonderful and awe inspiring. At times I could sense my soul, my consciousness granted a peek behind the veil, to say it was joyous would be an understatement. Many of life's mysteries were revealed and I now see the world in a way I could never have thought possible. This absolutely is a bittersweet journey but it's also one I wouldn't change, and despite everything, I wouldn't change Sarah either.

It's my honour that if any of my experiences mean that it helps just one other single soul, then for me it's worth it.

If you are a twin flame or think you may be then you have my admiration and respect, this is not a journey for the faint of heart. Some twins have to keep marriages, jobs, families and all sorts together whilst going through this. Some people are only revealed to be twins after their twin dies, like in the film i origins. Yes, this is how dramatic this is, twins will actually die for one another to invoke a spiritual awakening, other twins communicate across the veil. This truly is the realm of what the normal world would call supernatural. Yet to us this is actually the norm.

So where to start with what I've learnt? How to piece it together, and what is it that's going to help you?

What's it all for?

The "why" behind the intense challenges and awakening experienced on the twin flame journey is a profound and often perplexing question. It can indeed feel like a form of punishment or as if we're being subjected to trials for no apparent reason. The purpose of being shown the connection and embarking on this journey is multifaceted.

At its core, this journey is about spiritual awakening. It's designed to prompt us to awaken to our true selves, to understand our divine nature, and to recognise the nature of our existence on Earth. The challenges and experiences encountered serve as catalysts for this awakening process. It's not a punishment, but rather a path to spiritual growth, enlightenment, and a deeper understanding of our place in the world.

In recent times, many individuals are undergoing similar awakenings, contributing to a significant shift in the Earth's transition. While this transition may be challenging, it's also a period of great spiritual growth and transformation for humanity as a whole.

We get shown. Without any question of a doubt, that we are souls having a human experience. You are not your body. You are not your ego. Even your sex and name. It's a role you are playing. A role you chose to play. Along with the characters in your life. Often as is the case for many twin flames, the biggest antagonist may well be the person who loves you the most. After all, if you are putting together a play. Wouldn't you want your best friend playing the arch villain alongside you as the hero?

That for me was the profound lesson – the realisation that many of the things we often prioritise, like having the best car, the nicest house, or punctuality at work, can be mere illusions in the grand scheme of life. What truly matters is how we treat one another, the compassion and kindness we extend to fellow human beings. These actions, often seemingly small, have a lasting and genuine impact on our lives and the lives of others. It's a reminder that the quality of our interactions and our capacity for empathy hold far more significance than material possessions or superficial pursuits.

For twin flames, the journey is about soul ascension – shedding the ego while existing in the dense realm we know as Earth. This is considered one of the most challenging places to incarnate. The more we resist letting go, the more we suffer, and we are left with no choice but to embrace the present and trust in the purpose our souls have come here to fulfil. Along this path, we are tested in numerous ways, often losing the material possessions and illusions that surround us.

That's not to say it's easy; in fact, it's far from it. Despite one's spiritual growth, the desire for earthly pleasures still exists. I'm not going to say no to a Bentley. However, the universe tends to prioritise spiritual growth and purpose over Bentleys (yes, I know boring universe).

My Own Lessons.

Reflecting on the past, I can see many of the lessons I needed to learn. I used to rely on displays of grandiosity, such as taking people on lavish holidays and paying for things, thinking that these were the actions expected of a man to earn affection. In reality, I lacked the self-love to understand that I was enough just as I was, and it's the small, heartfelt gestures that hold the most significance.

I attempted to control my feelings with my ego and allowed fear to dictate my actions. I believed I needed societal validation through position, money, power, and material possessions to solidify my place in society. But I've come to realise that in a society that is often broken and materialistic, these external trappings are never enough to fill the void within.

Peace indeed comes from within, and much like we can't stop the rain from falling, we often can't change our external surroundings. Instead of trying to control the external world, we can change ourselves, much like donning a coat to protect us from the rain. When we make this internal shift, external circumstances lose their power over us, and we can even welcome life's challenges and storms.

94

So, rather than attempting to change others, it's more fruitful to focus on self-transformation. This process might entail a material cost, but it's important to remember that much of what we perceive as reality is, in fact, an illusion, and true peace and contentment are found within.

I have very little now in terms of material possessions, position in society, and very few good friends. Much of my time is spent alone, but it's in solitude that we connect with source, and in that connection we are never alone.

Why Is It So hard?

Probably the most asked question when it comes to spirituality and the soul's experience, and especially when it comes to the question of god, he seems like a right ole bugger doesn't he ? Putting us into this mess.

Each and every one of you is an incredibly powerful divine being, regardless of whether you're lounging on your sofa, indulging in the last cookie from a family pack, watching daytime TV wallowing in shame. You are a divine and potent entity, cherished and loved by souls who are even closer to you than your own family could ever hope to be.

It doesn't feel like it most of the time though, does it? Bills to pay, idiots cutting you up in traffic, social media full of bots, taxes on the rise and the boss is a bastard. Add to that the suffering of the drug addicts and homeless we see in the cities, reminding us there is even further to drop than where we are, and half the time that feels like a precarious hold.

The best way I can put it, is you've joined the navy seal of challenges, and that is planet earth, to incarnate as a human with its big ole ego, and man is that ego big. It takes us to our death before we even consider it isn't actually us.

In other words you didn't come to earth to have it easy, you came to earth because it's tough, because it's rough and because your soul benefits hugely from experiencing some of the toughest challenges there are. You are an infinite being, you can't die because death isn't a thing, time is a construct of this realm that we, along with the divine creator, made. And how spectacular is that ? Look around you, this is what you had a hand in making (well many of us did anyway)

Asking why life is full of suffering is a bit like complaining you're being shouted at when joining the army. You don't join the army and then are surprised because someone hurt your feelings a bit. That doesn't mean to say you can't complain and bitch about it, of course you can, and there's a lot to bitch about at times.

We willingly dive into some of life's most formidable challenges with the intention of transmuting their energies into divine love. However, success in this endeavour isn't guaranteed on the first attempt; it might take several tries. Along the way, we gather valuable lessons. Our path is a mix of pre-planned aspects and the exercise of free will.

In the words of Gandalf, "It's not always down to us what happens, what is down to us is how we deal with it." You've chosen the challenges you face today, regardless of how unfair, harsh, or dastardly life may have treated you. Your belief in making it through, despite the odds, is a testament to your strength and resilience.

A scene in a film I think explains everything so well is Les Miserables, when Jean Valjean steals the silverware from the bishop who treated him so kindly, the gendarmerie catches him and bring him back to the church. Almost with contempt they state that the culprit claimed the bishop had given him the silverware, with one word from the bishop Jean Valjean would have spent the rest of his life in prison. Instead, he says "Yes, that right, but brother you left so early, surely something slipped your mind, you forgot these candlesticks, would you leave the best behind" and with those candlesticks many a life was changed for the better.

The candlesticks are an illusion, the good the bishop did was not.

It makes me question if I could ever rise to be as magnanimous as the bishop, capable of forgiving those who wronged me, when trying to do them good, and not only forgiving but also loving and caring for those who have caused harm.

So often though, we are Jean Valjean, searching for others to understand us, and give us the break we so often don't give ourselves.

These lessons are not easy to learn; they often take a lifetime to truly internalise. It's one thing to write about forgiveness and share inspirational memes on social media, but it's an entirely different challenge to live these principles day in and day out. It's a lifelong journey of growth and self-discovery.

I slip, for sure I slip, we are dealing with being human after all, and life is not a scripted play with a known ending. It's the unknown that causes fear.

I get asked many questions about twin flames. So I thought I'd cover the most popular. If this ends up being popular then I'll expand on it.

What Are Twin Flames?

The first thing to understand is what you are, without accepting or understanding that you are indeed a soul with a human body, well, twin flames make no sense. I so often see people confuse the term for a love relationship without really considering what it actually means.

Your twin flame is another soul who resonates with the exact same soul frequency as you do. However, it's important to understand that they are not yours, nor do they belong to you. They are a distinct consciousness, but they share your soul's frequency. Despite this shared frequency, they often manifest as almost the complete opposite of you, which makes the connection fascinating. It's not merely a matter of "opposites attract"; in many ways, they can be very different from you in their outward expression.

Can You Be Married to a Twin and Not Know It?

I'm going to encapsulate all these kinds of questions in one. The answer is no one really knows, I have little doubts that many twins may have incarnated together to lead happy, peaceful loving lives on Earth. But if you aren't meant to know you are twins, well then you just don't know. On earth it's your soulmates that you generally walk lockstep through life with.

Many individuals who claim to be in a twin flame union may, in fact, be in a soulmate connection. It's crucial to recognise that while we are all connected in a broader sense as soulmates, there is indeed a specific soul family or soul group to which we belong. In reality, finding true twin flames in a genuine union can be quite rare.

It's not to say that true twin flame unions are impossible, but the current cycle on Earth means it's not time for playing happy bunnies and snuggles. Twin flame connections often involve deep spiritual growth and significant challenges that must be overcome, this in turn helps with the vibration of the collective here on earth. We may be a small part of the puzzle, but indeed we are an important part.

How Can I Meet My Twin Flame ?

If you read this and still want to meet your twin? You're nuts. But the fact is if you know about twins, then you won't meet them, we reside in a dimension where twin flames don't exist. And yes we absolutely shift dimensions. The multiverse is real and you live in it.

You may well have a twin flame. An eternal partner. In fact, everyone may have one. But this life isn't for that journey. That doesn't mean to say you can't awaken spirituality by any means. There are plenty of ways the ego can get battered in this amusement park of a planet.

How Do I Know If Someone Is My Twin?

None of us had any prior concept of twin flames or soulmates, and we certainly didn't actively pursue the spiritual awakening that eventually unfolded. This isn't something you can seek out; rather, it's something that is revealed to you in extraordinary and often paranormal ways, guided by a higher power or force, whether you call it God, the universe, spirit, the flying spaghetti monster.

Awakened twin flames often come to this journey with a wealth of life experiences, having navigated through toxic relationships, obsessions with others, and being the object of someone else's obsession. The journey is not akin to the love-struck experiences of teenagers that can be easily dismissed with a simple "get over it." It's a complex, profound, and transformative process that encompasses many facets of life, and it often takes time and introspection to fully comprehend and navigate. Twin flames who have weathered the storm of life's challenges bring unique insights and resilience to their journey.

Basically the universe will tell you, it's unmistakable, not a few crows, or a few feathers, for many of us it's like we are plucked out of our lives and held down until we accept the connection. And it's insane.

How Do I Get My Twin Flame Back?

This question arises so frequently, and the answer is quite clear. Firstly, it's essential to understand that your twin flame is not truly "yours" in the way many people believe. Many envision a mystical bond that unites the two of you against the world, but the reality often feels more like a tumultuous relationship than an idyllic one. It's not uncommon to see many twin flames feeling exhausted, battered, and broken on this journey.

The crucial lesson is that you must heal for yourself, and yourself alone. Only when you fully grasp that this journey is about your personal growth, not dependent on anyone else, will things begin to improve. At that point, you won't need or long for your twin flame. It may sound harsh, but it's the path toward personal salvation and growth.

If you find yourself at a point where you still yearn for your twin flame to return, it's an indication that there are more lessons and personal growth to be experienced on your journey. However, it's worth noting that regardless of whether or not someone is your twin flame, investing in your own healing and personal development is a valuable and rewarding endeavour. Self-healing and growth are essential steps on the path to a more fulfilled and balanced life.

In short, we lose all expectations, we try not to put our heels in the ground and say never again (I learnt that one) and we don't wish they would return. It just is.

Is It Possible That My Twin Dies Before I Know?

This one seems brutal, but the answer is yes. There are many people who find out that it was their twin after their death. They can reach out beyond the veil, after all, most of us experience our twin's higher self. The lesson for each of us though, is the same.

What About Celebrity Twin Flames

Yeah, just no, the ones proclaiming the are twin flames in matching sweaters make us want to hurl as well.

Final Word

This is a book predominately about spirituality, it has taken me years to basically realise everything we need is truly within us. That it's the small things that count, not the big gestures. If you don't feel "spiritual enough" well that's fine, you're not meant to, it doesn't make you any less spiritual, after all we are all spiritual beings. Your path in life is as important as anyone else's, you are no more or no less than any other soul incarnated. In fact, so often it's those that have taken on the most challenging roles in society that are the more advanced souls. I'm sorry to say it's unlikely many old souls incarnate with big trust funds and a heated swimming pool. More likely a cardboard box and a car park puddle.

You don't have to believe in anything, a god, a creator, or that twins exist at all. There is no fiery hell for your beliefs, you choose to incarnate without them.

The main thing above all else, the most important thing to always remember, be kind to yourself and others. And if you can't be kind, try not to make others' lives harder. Everything else you can figure out as you go.

It's rough and tough out there, but you can do it.

This book is written with thanks to other twins who kindly read the book for their feedback. My love to all those on this most tumultuous of journeys.